POWER TO DOMINATE

The mental process involved in convincing

John B. Bricker

DISCLAIMER

DEDICATION

I dedicate this book to my brother for his patience and understanding, while writing this book I had issues with my laptop and he gave me his laptop not minding that he had his own work to finish, I really appreciate you bro.

Table of Contents

INTRODUCTION

To have the option to cause somebody to accomplish something since you said so or meant through implicit words with next to no type of brutality or treat to life is called predominance, or ability to overwhelm. Persuasive individuals rule their current circumstance/environmental elements for sure however Strength is fleeting because of many reasons, a model is the resistance delighted in by a serving lead representative or president in America which is stopped after they leave office.

As ordered progressions and layers lessen, creating individual adequacy and it is crucial for impact abilities. Achievement and results must be accomplished through, with and from others. Having the option to impact without formal authority is a fundamental ability, and we can't do this without certainty, clearness of direction and the relational abilities to articulate our thoughts completely. In addition, our roles as leaders necessitate that we draw on both our personal qualities and our actions to motivate and engage our employees. Skills for influence go beyond simply persuading others to always share our viewpoint; we can also influence them to cooperate with us and not always do so. It's not necessary to focus on succeeding no matter what and getting our own specific manner constantly. There's actually no need to focus on compelling or getting others to transform, we can't transform others.

Affecting abilities is tied in with acting in manners that offers others the challenge to change their way of behaving, mentalities, considerations, and ways as well as oblige your own desires while tolerating that they might not be able to or reluctant to, or are ill-equipped to meet our solicitation to be impacted.

The fact of the matter is that we constantly employ our influencing abilities, not just through our actions, whether we like it or not. Our very presence at a gathering might impact individuals decidedly or adversely. The style or nature of our presence, what we say or how we say it and the mentality we unknowingly or in any case project says a lot.

Personally, we can become more powerful and effective the more knowledgeable we are about what we do and how it affects others.

Have you ever been affected by someone else? It could be your parents, a coach, a mentor, a friend, or even a colleague at work. Impacting is tied in with doing things that you are great at, and that implies you can impact somebody without affecting them adversely. All things considered, it is finished so that the individual is impacted without acknowledging he is being affected.

Being powerful working can assist you with making individual progress by permitting you to be an extraordinary pioneer and accomplish corporate targets. Building impacting capacities can assist you with convincing colleagues to help your points and thoughts by empowering and convincing them. We'll go over what they are, how to use them, and how to improve your influencing abilities.

Impact is something that comes into various parts of our lives, and more often than not we aren't even mindful of it. Everything from the buys we make to individuals we gaze upward to at work is a result of impact, and the capacity to impact others ourselves can be exceptionally valuable in a wide assortment of circumstances.

However, this capacity is certainly not a singular expertise in itself. Arranging and impacting abilities are really an entire scope of various traits and capacities, some of which are not difficult to embrace and some of which will require some investment to dominate.

Impacting is characterized as the interaction by which an individual can change or influence the assessments of others. In the event that somebody is depicted as having impact, it ordinarily implies that their mentalities and thoughts are regarded and upheld by others and that they frequently obtain the results they need from circumstances.

Direct persuasion is more about arguing and persuading someone else to change their mind, whereas influencing people is more about expressing your own point of view in a manner that inspires others to adopt the same mindset. Impacting for the most part works by acting such that others perceive and regard, rather than effectively going out and imparting your insights to make others adjust theirs.

The capacity to impact is much of the time an expertise that is credited to pioneers and those in a, strategic, influential place, however it is quite simple for anybody to master impacting procedures and abilities to emit a positive impression and get others to admire them. This is an exceptionally gainful expertise to have from an expert perspective, especially in jobs like group pioneer, coach or specialist.

Impacting abilities join a significant number of the perspectives expected in great correspondence, exchange and influence. A wide range of abilities will emphatically affect your capacity to impact others, the most significant of which are point by point underneath.

SHARE

Sharing or reciprocating is the first universal principle of influence.

People esteem fairness and equilibrium somewhat. This implies we could do without to feel that we owe others. As a rule, individuals have these social commitments they attempt to settle them. For instance, on the off chance that somebody sends you a birthday card, you'll more likely than not have any desire to send them one consequently. In order to satisfy your sense of social obligation, you will carry out this action when their birthday comes around again.

It's feasible to involve this longing for correspondence to impact the ways of behaving of others.

 Somewhat, the worth of the gift is less vital that the demonstration of the actual gift. For this reason of reciprocity, wait staff may include mints in the bill, workshop facilitators may offer cookies when soliciting feedback, and leaders may offer a team outing just prior to distributing the annual engagement survey. These activities essentially say, "I've taken care of you, presently you scratch mine".

In the realm of work it's feasible to utilize this guideline of correspondence by offering courtesies to other people, helping individuals, openly commending others and by and large working so as to develop a bank of social commitments owed to you. At some point, each of these responsibilities will be settled, probably to your advantage. Of course, this kind of behavior will cease to be effective if you go overboard with it.

The Offer/correspondence standard is a strong mental device that can assist you with impacting others and fabricate trust. In view of the thought individuals feel obliged to return favors and treat others as they have been dealt with. In this book, you will figure out how to utilize the correspondence guideline to further develop your administration abilities and accomplish your objectives.

Reciprocity is a human need as well as a social norm. We are wired to look for equilibrium and reasonableness in our connections, and we will more often than not stay away from the people who exploit or disregard us. At the point when you practice correspondence, you extend regard, appreciation, and liberality to other people, which thus make them bound to coordinate, support, and respond your activities. This makes a positive pattern of trust and impact that can help the two players.

Correspondence can be a compelling method for impacting others, so the following are a couple of tips to remember. Begin by being proactive and starting the trade with something significant, like a commendation, suggestion, reference, or arrangement. Ensure that what you offer is pertinent to the next individual's inclinations, necessities, and objectives. When you receive something from others, be sincere and genuine in your actions and words. Moreover, responding on time is significant; the more you stand by, the less effect your signal will have. Attempt to coordinate or surpass the worth and speed of what you have gotten so the other individual won't feel neglected or underestimated.

Reciprocity can have both good and bad sides. Whenever utilized accurately, it can build your initiative and impact, yet whenever utilized inappropriately; it can make the contrary difference and harm your standing. It is critical to know about typical traps to stay away from them. For example, don't offer excessively or again and again, as this could make an awareness of certain expectations or obligation, making the other individual feels awkward or angry. On the other hand, you shouldn't give too little or too often, or you might come across as stingy or unappreciative. Moreover, don't involve correspondence as a method for controlling or pressure others; this will bring about you losing their trust and regard. Eventually, you need to be viewed as somebody who provides for fabricate compatibility and steadfastness with others, not somebody who just gets and never gives.

Correspondence is certainly not a one-time occasion, yet a drawn out procedure. To assess its viability, you want to track and gauge its outcomes over the long haul. You ought to search for pointers like expanded commitment - are individuals you collaborate with more responsive, mindful, and involved? Do they show more interest and energy in your thoughts, ventures, and objectives? Furthermore, further developed connections - are individuals you collaborate with more well disposed, strong, and steadfast? Do they extend more regard, appreciation, and acknowledgment for your commitments and accomplishments? Ultimately, upgraded results - are individuals you interface with really willing, capable, and persuaded to assist you with accomplishing your objectives? Do they offer you additional resources, information, and advice to help you succeed?

Correspondence is definitely not an inherent expertise for everybody, except it very well may be learned and improved with training. To foster your correspondence abilities, notice and gain from instances of correspondence in real life. Try out a variety of approaches to implementing reciprocity in various contexts and adapt your strategy to the person, the objective, and the context. Consider your activities and results routinely, and distinguish your assets and shortcomings. Look for input from others, and integrate their ideas into your activity intends to work on your abilities. With these tips, you can utilize correspondence to impact others, assemble trust, improve your authority, and accomplish your objectives.

THE ART OF AWARENESS/OBSERVATION

Many individuals go into discussions, either because of an absence of certainty or indifference, and others go into a discussion zeroed in soundly on what they ask for from it. Very few individuals invest energy at first to peruse the room, understanding what drives individuals around them, and where they can offer worth. This HBR article about perusing the room is a decent one.

Correspondence offers us all the chance to acquire information, experiences, and understanding. At the point when you listen effectively to individuals around you (not looking at snooping), and you watch them mindfully while they are approaching their bustling lives, you realize what is most important to them, what is vital to them, and where you might actually help. Keep in mind, helping other people assembles your renown.

What to Notice

The short response is "as much as humanly conceivable". Your communication style and content will be more tailored the more you know about the people around you. Utilize your eyes and ears to check for important experiences about everybody you are going to meet. At the point when you have perused the room, you will actually want to zero in additional on what you know and less on your instinct about individuals. Try not to misunderstand me, instinct is significant down the line, yet it can cause you problems when it drives you to profound choices, so working with realities will guard you.

The following are a couple of devices to utilize while noticing others:

Undivided attention

It has been said that we as a whole have two ears and one mouth, so use them relatively. You realize when you tune in; not really when you talk. It is likewise essentially vital that you are really keen on what the other individual is talking about. It is useless to simply stay there trusting that your turn will talk. Showing interest, genuine interest in what somebody is referring to, makes you more fascinating to the speaker.

We are so desensitized to prearranged discussions that we will generally daydream a piece when taken part in proficient/business discussions, yet when you stray off-script and ask something out of private interest, and you then tune in with interest, it lifts the mist and the speaker wakes up from auto-pilot. You become critical and fascinating. This is a foundation of building a strong individual/proficient connection with somebody. Everybody has "war stories" to share, and you can glean some useful knowledge from them. It gives you a way to learn a lot about the people you work with and many great insights.

Keep an open mind, lest you be judged! It's a Christian staple, however an excellent rule in the viable correspondence world. Receptiveness is basic to basic and levelheaded reasoning. You can gain positive bits of knowledge from even the most unlikable characters in the event that you simply keep a receptive outlook. You have the power and command over what you realize. Keep in mind, you are mindful and realize your guiding principle and convictions, and you pick your ways of behaving.

At the point when participated in a discussion, make a move to pay attention to what the other individual is talking about, regardless of whether you concur with the substance. The experiences shared will educate you a ton regarding the other individual, and that is the thing you need. You need to understand what makes him/her tick, what kinds of words and points trigger him/her. Your prestige and positive influence will rise as a result of this knowledge, which will enable you to have more meaningful conversations in the future.

Back to what to notice. Indeed, even before you take part in a discussion with somebody, stand back and watch for the accompanying things:

Characteristics

This is a fascinating one; as such a huge amount in correspondence lives in non-verbal communication. You can learn more about a person by watching how they move and interact with the things and people around them than you can by listening to what they say. You could check his/her profound state, mindfulness, different preferences, thus significantly more. Watching somebody move might let you know if he/she is a loner, outgoing individual, or ambivert.

Motivating forces

While noticing others, common sense would suggest that we should comprehend what is critical to them with regards to acquire. Not all individuals feel boosted to get things done for similar reasons you do. You could like extra energy and any choice that will give you all the more leisure time will be focused on by you, however the individual close to you could like cash as well as material things more and will focus on choices in light of what things he/she can get from going with a choice. Noticing individuals in your own and proficient life, and seeing them light up or diminish down while engaged with conversations, will enlighten you more regarding where their impetus inclinations lie.

Energy

Energy drives us! While noticing somebody's energy throughout everyday life, you can obviously see it in their non-verbal communication and peculiarities. Additionally, it gives you the chance to discover shared interests with the other person, which can be used to tailor your conversation to make it more meaningful and memorable for both of you.

It's vital to call attention to that you don't must have precisely the same enthusiasm as the individual you are in discussion with to relate. Numerous interests, similar to enterprises, have points of convergence. A simple illustration of this would be the playing of instruments. You could play the guitar and the other individual could play the piano. The convergence of the two is music. I know that is an exceptionally essential model; however I'm certain you get the point. In reality, here's another model. You may be a muscular specialist and the other individual is a mechanical designer. These are two totally various callings and fields; notwithstanding, they meet at the purpose in designing. Finding the convergence between your energy and another person's will build the profundity of your discussions and the valuable open doors for acquiring experiences.

Certainty

Noticing somebody's degree of certainty is perfect for measuring his/her receptiveness to a liquid discussion. Frequently, when somebody displays high certainty, they are fiery and responsive to discussions and they are probably going to share experiences.

Then again, in the event that somebody shows an absence of certainty, they are probably going to be less disposed to go into a discussion and to share bits of knowledge. This doesn't imply that you ought to stay away from individuals with low certainty. The observation alone reveals the appropriate manner of interaction to engage in with another individual. Applying a high energy style could be overpowering to somebody with low certainty levels, so a superior methodology is to pose inquiries that will assist the individual with grasping his/her worth. A model would be, asking him/her about something that he/she does consistently and is great at, which, while he/she is discussing it, will develop their certainty. This is a type of positive impact and will assist you with building distinction according to your partners and friends.

Profound state

This one needn't bother with a great deal of clarification yet it accompanies an admonition. There is a scarcely discernible difference among EQ and Instinct. Checking somebody close to home state ought to be relevant and directed inside before you rush to make judgment calls. The capacity to understand people at their core (EQ) is put together a ton with respect to life experience and cautious investigation. Noticing somebody and deciding their close to home state on what you see right now, without grasping the ecological impacts that prompted that state, isn't protected. Take into consideration a person's behavior and emotional state in the past. Now, this caution mostly applies in situations where the person is feeling bad. To be useful to him/her in a discussion, find out about the wellspring of the aggravation goes quite far.

A person who exudes a positive emotional state indicates that they will be an energetic and upbeat participant in a conversation. This could be valuable to you, as it will assist you with acquiring close to home energy when you want it, and bringing the individual into a gathering discussion will meaningfully affect the gathering. Positive feelings and energy spread as a natural by-product, without a doubt!

When and Where to Notice

When would it be advisable for you to notice individuals around you? Always! The more you notice, the more you learn, and the more you learn, the more educated and set you up are. You shouldn't take it all the way up to the Stalker-Level, I suppose. This carries us to "Where would it be advisable for you to notice?" You ought to notice individuals around you any place you are normally. This could be working around the workplace, at home around your family, and at get-togethers ideally where you were welcome to.

In Synopsis

Your observational abilities and your certified interest in others are essential to your life as a talented expert. Care about others and their idiosyncrasies, interests, and close to home states. Listen effectively to what individuals are talking about and consistently keep a receptive outlook. This will assist you with acquiring significant bits of knowledge into a horde of various enterprises and callings, and will develop your distinction and powers of positive impact. Utilizing your powers of observation is the most effective method for crowdsourcing information.

LISTENING

In our own and proficient life, we are for the most part doing one thing for example "correspondence." In our day to day proficient routine we are collaborating with one another, compromising guidelines, selling and promoting administrations, working with different divisions, going to gatherings, directing, preparing, talking with others, pursuing business choices on verbal correspondence, , haggling with clients and so forth.

Here explicitly I might want to zero in on the up close and personal correspondence.

How might we Impact others with our listening abilities?

We do one specific thing, either intentionally or unintentionally, when communicating, especially when negotiating with clients: is to communicate to other people "our" viewpoint. Most extreme level of the time is used for it, to settle the negotiation in support of ourselves. In the associations, representative administration worker collaboration happens like clockwork.

Then, at that point, for what reason would it be advisable for us to listen more than talking?

The inquiry emerges why we ought to tune in; as for the most part the typical day to day drill is to talk really for convincing or causing others to acknowledge our perspective. On account of business contracts while haggling to settle the negotiation, we feature center around our viewpoint. In this situation, we frequently believe that one should be able to influence the audience well to keep the stage. Be that as it may, listening ability assume a significant part in going with key business choice which is disregarded at times.

Listening abilities generally increment our focus and lead to mutual benefit circumstance in business matters. We listen well; we come up with a better solution and learn more from the discussions.

In consistent picking up, listening abilities, consistently assumes a vital part. Being a decent audience can expand our responsibility towards our work, consequently empower us to comprehend what is happening precisely and keeps us mindful of what is happening in the division/association.

When we pay attention to what they have to say, people start to like us internally. They feel great while talking about business related issues as well as private matters as well. A decent conversation prompts improved certainty, and they achieve the inner harmony and feel battled.

Our responses are more likely to adapt to the situation, alleviate the situation for others, and project an intelligent, practical response for them when we listen attentively.

By listening well, we can improve our working relationships with others. Recall a decent audience generally looks for and find the underlying driver of an issue, making it simpler to tackle it. Since data holds with audience and most arrangements are consistently inside the issue.

Challenge: In our everyday daily practice in business/office climate, might we at any point provoke ourselves to go through a functioning day 80% tuning in and 20% talking? At day's end, assess what you gain, and see the distinction. It will represent itself with no issue.

We generally focus while paying attention to other people, finding the significant components in the discussion, knowing the feelings of others, making a decision about the speaker's character. While the speaker looks to impart things to you, audience constructs their certainty level; compassion constructs shared regards, speaker looks for guidance and takes genuine assessment on issues. I quote Larry Wilson here that "One ought to be an expert of Human Relations."

At any point as a manager, do we imagine that assuming we listen well to a worker who is feeling demotivated, confounded, yet subsequent to imparting contemplations to you he/she feel loose and agreeable until the end of the day. Consider esteem expansion in the efficiency it brings. Keep in mind that positive energy always emanates from speakers who are attentive.

Non-verbal communication is likewise a vital variable for growing great listening abilities. We need to visually connect, keep recognizing and understand discussion; pose inquiries for specific explanations and give positive input. Individual quirk is vital as well. For instance we ought to figure out how to stay away from the specific individual propensities or acts while tuning in, e.g., waving hand, seeing to a great extent, gnawing the lips, playing with pen, ties, hairs and so on. It is an interruption.

In conference, addresses, gathering individuals take notes more often than not. This is a decent practice itself however at some point we fail to remember the central issues of the speaker while we take notes. When the propensity for great listening creates, it improves our reaction, empowering us to hold explicit substantial data and foster a superior comprehension of the subject.

Presently envision that during the discussion, the individual you're addressing is browsing email, flipping through a scratch pad, or messaging ceaselessly on their cell. Or then again, imagine a scenario where the individual in question continues intruding on or differing before you're ready to make your total point.

It's staggeringly disappointing, however tragically, it happens constantly. No mystery listening has become more enthusiastically than any time in recent memory in the present working environment. Every minute of the day, there are so many devices, notifications, and gadgets that beg for our attention that we frequently fool ourselves into thinking that they are more important than a conversation that is taking place right in front of us.

Additionally, we face a biological problem: We can tune in multiple times quicker than anybody can talk. That implies we have abundance limit in our mind that will stray and engage itself except if we do whatever it takes to oversee it deliberately.

When you figure out how to do that, in any case, you'll genuinely support your value in the workplace.

FEEDBACK

Criticism is one of the most important ways of convincing and impacts others in your association or family or even your regular experiences with individuals. Whether you are a pioneer, a supervisor, a partner, or a client, you can utilize criticism to influence conduct, further develop execution, construct trust, and cultivate coordinated effort. Nonetheless, criticism is definitely not a one-size-fits-all device. You want to know how to give and get input really, and how to adjust your criticism style to various circumstances and individuals.

Before you give input, you should be clear about what you need to accomplish. Would you like to adulate, right, mentor, propel, or challenge somebody? Would you like to share data, assumptions, suppositions, or sentiments? Would you like to impact a choice, a way of behaving, or a relationship? Your motivation will decide the substance, tone, and timing of your criticism, as well as the response you anticipate from the collector.

Criticism can be given in various ways, for example, verbally, recorded as a hard copy, or through signals and activities. Every strategy enjoys its benefits and hindrances, contingent upon the specific situation and the message. Verbal feedback, for instance, can be more immediate, personal, and direct than written feedback, but it can also be more prone to misunderstandings, emotions, and interruptions. While written feedback can be more impersonal, delayed, and rigid, it can also be more detailed, structured, and documented. Gestures and actions can be more ethereal, spontaneous, and expressive, but they can also be hazier, inconsistent, and misunderstood. You want to pick the technique that best suits your motivation, your crowd, and your circumstance.

Criticism is more enticing and compelling when it is explicit and concrete, as opposed to obscure and general. Explicit and substantial input alludes to discernible realities, ways of behaving, and results, as opposed to translations, decisions, and presumptions. It additionally gives models, proof, and information, as opposed to suppositions, sentiments, and impressions. Explicit and substantial criticism assists the recipient with understanding what you are talking about, why you are saying it, and what you believe that they should do.

Input is more convincing and persuasive when it is positive and productive, as opposed to negative and horrendous. Positive and productive criticism centers on qualities, open doors, and arrangements, as opposed to shortcomings, issues, and blames. It likewise recognizes accomplishments, endeavors, and progress, as opposed to disappointments, slip-ups, and holes. Good and productive input assists the recipient with feeling esteemed, regarded, and roused, as opposed to censured, accused, and deterred.

Input is more enticing and powerful when it is predictable and congruent, as opposed to problematic and incongruent. Feedback that is consistent and in line with your goals, strategy and message is good. It likewise coordinates with the beneficiary's assumptions, necessities, and objectives. Predictable and compatible criticism assists the collector with confiding in you, to follow you, and to help out you.

Criticism is certainly not a one-way correspondence, however a two-way exchange. You must be open and receptive to both the feedback you give to others and the feedback you receive from others. Being open and responsive means listening effectively, clarifying pressing issues, looking for explanation, showing appreciation, and communicating understanding or conflict deferentially. It additionally implies following up on the criticism, carrying out changes, looking for input once more, and showing improvement. Being open and responsive assists you with gaining from others, to work on yourself, and to impact others.

SELF CONFIDENCE AS A MOTIVATOR

A powerful quality that can have a significant impact on our lives is confidence. It goes past having confidence in ourselves; it incorporates confidence and individual strength. At the point when we have certainty, we transmit inspiration, conquer difficulties with beauty, and move everyone around us. However, what precisely is certainty and for what reason is it so significant in self-improvement?

Figuring out Certainty

Certainty is frequently misjudged, seen as something that certain individuals normally have while others battle to find. In any case, truly, certainty is a mastered expertise that can be developed and sustained. It is the confidence in one's capacities and worth, permitting people to embrace their uniqueness and stand tall despite misfortune.

Characterizing Certainty and its Significance in self-improvement Certainty can be characterized as a perspective where people trust in their own capacities and have a positive perspective on themselves. It assumes an essential part in self-awareness as it enables people to seek after objectives, face challenges, and get out of their usual ranges of familiarity. We are more likely to take advantage of opportunities when we are confident. Certainty isn't restricted to a solitary part of life. It penetrates through different spaces, including profession, connections, and self-awareness. In the expert domain, certainty empowers people to champion themselves, share their thoughts, and take on positions of authority. In connections, certainty considers open correspondence, weakness, and the capacity to define solid limits. In self-improvement, certainty powers the longing to learn, investigate new encounters, and persistently work on oneself.

The Brain research behind Fearlessness and Confidence

Certainty is well established in brain research, entwined with confidence. Self-confidence focuses on specific areas of competence and belief, while self-esteem refers to an individual's overall opinion of themselves. In order to establish a solid foundation for personal development and resilience, both are essential.

Self-assurance is definitely not a proper quality however can vary contingent upon different elements.

It is affected by our viewpoints, feelings, and encounters. For instance, getting positive input and achieving objectives can support our certainty, while negative encounters or analysis can challenge it. Understanding the brain research behind fearlessness permits us to foster methodologies to upgrade it and keep a sound degree of confidence.

Factors Affecting Certainty: Climate, Childhood, and Encounters.

Certainty can be molded by different elements, including our current circumstance, childhood, and previous encounters. Experiencing childhood in a steady and empowering climate can cultivate a healthy identity conviction, while negative encounters or basic criticism can challenge our certainty. But it's important to remember that these external factors aren't the only thing that affects confidence. With mindfulness and purposeful exertion, people can beat past difficulties and foster areas of strength for self-assurance.

Moreover, individuals we encircle ourselves with can fundamentally influence our certainty. Positive and steady connections can elevate and motivate us, while poisonous or unsupportive connections can sabotage our self-conviction. By developing an organization of people who have faith in our capacities and energize our development, we can establish a climate that sustains and improves our certainty.

The Connection between Confidence and Mental Health

There is a strong connection between confidence and mental health. At the point when we have low fearlessness, it can add to sensations of uneasiness, self-uncertainty, and discouragement. On the other hand, increasing our level of confidence can benefit our overall health. By focusing on our emotional wellness and doing whatever it may take to develop certainty, we can make a strong starting point for self-improvement. Building certainty includes testing negative idea designs, rehearsing self-empathy, and looking for help when required. Participating in exercises that line up with our qualities and assets can likewise help our certainty and give a feeling of motivation. By focusing on taking care of oneself and supporting our psychological well-being, we can make a positive cycle where certainty and prosperity build up one another.

Conquering an inability to acknowledge success and Self-Uncertainty.

An inability to embrace success, a sensation of not meriting our achievements or dreading being uncovered as a fake, is a typical hindrance to certainty. Numerous people, regardless of their accomplishments, battle with self-question and a diligent feeling of dread toward being "found out." Figuring out how to perceive and defeat self-question is an essential move toward developing bona fide certainty. Reframing our thoughts and concentrating on our accomplishments and strengths is one effective method for overcoming impostor syndrome. By recognizing our accomplishments and crediting them to our abilities and difficult work, we can fabricate a more precise and positive self-insight. Mentors, friends, and therapists can also help us confront our self-doubt and offer helpful perspective.

Famous Hypotheses of Fearlessness

With these definitions close by, we can investigate normal convictions and famous hypotheses encompassing fearlessness and confidence.

There are speculations and systems for figuring out confidence in the mental writing however I will name a couple.

Maslow's Order of Requirements

Maslow's order of requirements, a famous albeit fairly obsolete structure in brain science, speculates that there are a few necessities that people probably met to be genuinely satisfied, at the same time, by and large, the most essential requirements should be met before additional mind boggling requirements can be met. Self-esteem, after self-actualization, is the second most important need in his pyramid.

As per Maslow, people should have their necessities of physiological dependability, security, love and having a place met before they can foster sound confidence. He likewise noticed that there are two sorts of confidence, a "higher" and a "lower," the lower confidence got from the admiration of others, while the higher confidence comes from the inside.

Soon after his presentation of the progressive system of necessities, Maslow refined his hypothesis to oblige the occurrences of profoundly self-completed individuals who are destitute or people who live in a perilous region or disaster area but on the other hand are high in confidence.

This pecking order is not generally thought to be as a severe hypothesis of unidirectional development, yet a more broad clarification of how essential requirements being met permit people the opportunity and capacity to accomplish their more complicated ones.

Terror Management Theory

A hazier hypothesis that digs a piece further into the human experience to make sense of self-assurance is the Dread Administration Hypothesis.

Terror Management Theory (TMT) depends on the possibility that people hold extraordinary potential for answering with dread to the consciousness of their own mortality, and those perspectives that stress people groups' convictions in their own importance as people safeguard them against this fear.

TMT sets that confidence structures as a method for safeguarding and cradle against tension, and hence, individuals take a stab at self-assurance and respond adversely to any person or thing that could subvert their convictions in their consoling perspective.

Sociometer Hypothesis

Mark Leary, a social clinician who explores confidence with regards to developmental brain research, likewise contributed a hypothesis of confidence to the writing.

The Sociometer Hypothesis recommends that confidence is an interior check of how much one is incorporated versus prohibited by others. This hypothesis lays on the origination of confidence as an inner individual impression of social acknowledgment and dismissal.

This theory's accuracy and applicability are supported by substantial evidence. For instance, studies have shown that the results of occasions on individuals' confidence by and large coordinate with their suppositions about how similar occasions would make others acknowledge or dismiss them.

At last, proof shows that social avoidance in view of individual qualities diminishes confidence.

Benefits

These advantages expand further and more extensive than a great many people understand. If you are a leader, manager, sales representative, or individual contributor, improving your self-confidence will benefit you professionally. It will help you actually by assisting you with driving your family and it even assists you with feeling and others to see you as hotter. Indeed, certainty is hot!

Being at your best even under pressure. Competitors, performers and entertainers will confirm the significance of an elevated degree of certainty. When you are self-assured, you are able to perform to your full potential, and you want to be at your best under pressure.

Affecting others. Self-assured individuals frequently impact others all the more promptly. This is helpful when negotiating at work or at home, selling an idea or a product, or both.

Having administration and chief presence. Fearlessness has a major impact in initiative and chief presence. You make such presence by your thought process, act counting how you convey your body and utilize your voice.

Radiating a more uplifting outlook. You have a more upbeat outlook when you are self-assured and believe you have a significant role to play in the world.

Feeling esteemed. At the point when you're sure, you understand what you succeed at and that you have esteem.

Ascending to success. Are you looking for a raise? The more certainty you have, the more probable you are to be advanced.

Decreasing negative contemplations. More noteworthy fearlessness permits you to encounter independence from self-uncertainty and negative considerations about yourself.

Feeling less anxious and more fearless. You are more able to step outside of your comfort zone and take calculated risks with greater confidence.

Having more noteworthy independence from social uneasiness. Turning out to be happier with acting naturally lessens worry about what others could imagine you. How freeing!

Acquiring energy and inspiration to make a move Certainty gives you sure energy to make a move to accomplish your own and proficient objectives and dreams. The more exceptionally energetic and empowered you are, the almost certain you are to make a quick move.

Being more joyful. People who lack self-confidence are more likely to be unhappy and dissatisfied with their lives than confident people.

COMMUNICATION - TIMING

So, when you decide to talk to someone, what leads you to believe that the time is right? Timing is pivotal to your correspondence, the explanation I express this is on the grounds that it will direct the setting. It goes about as an outstanding multiplier for other correspondence properties (like tone, information, thought process, etc). So while perusing this consider timing a genuinely sizeable multiplier to anything that correspondence property you're hoping to approach with.

So we should separate it, time itself is a variable inside an endless space to the individual and its specialized definition

I will not be unraveling the profound implications behind the abovementioned; However, the key word "events," which refers to the occurrences in an individual's life over a predetermined time period (past, present, or potential future), is what we are focusing on here. This is critical to knowing while the timing is correct; this is clearly easy to talk about, not so easy to do, as you are no clairvoyant. So you have somewhat of a situation finding out when something is suitable to make reference to this person.

There are a large number of elements you can notice and compute to sort out what express the individual is in. Perception is the fundamental apparatus, whether it is with your eyes or ears. A few guides to give you...

- Notice assuming they have quite recently completed the process of addressing somebody, whether by telephone or eye to eye. Recognize the recipient's identity and consider the potential effects on their state.

• Take note of the time of day; could this affect how they respond? For example on the off chance that they've recently awakened and it's 5am, is it the best opportunity to pop off the subject of 'will you wed me?' Although this is a straightforward illustration, you get the point.

• Pay attention to how they talk to other people. If it's at work, pay attention to how they respond to other people. Like tone, jargon and intention. Regardless of whether it's in the family a similar rule applies

•   Perusing the people face, this variable is a piece interesting as a matter of fact not every person can peruse, comprehend and interpret look and self-restraint.

There are a lot of other things that influence when the timing is right, including the ones listed above. The more exertion you put in noticing the people express the simpler it becomes to raise a ruckus around town 'spot' concerning timing.

So we've examined one portion of the issue, which is understanding the condition of an individual, the other half is gauging the effect. So you've felt free to speak with the singular what will be the result from your activities. It's similarly as significant comprehension the ramifications from addressing somebody for all intents and purposes to plan. The explanation I express that is on the grounds that discourse is recoverable and the pardoning esteem is genuinely high on the scale.

So on the off chance that you mess up your discourse, or have drawn nearer with some unacceptable tone or realities it's reversible with some elegance. As I already mentioned, being able to observe and read the situation is crucial for timing because it enables you to perform the same "post-mortem" on your discussion.

You as need might arise to notice the response given by individual you are conversing with. There are by and by a huge number of perceptions to search for in a post-response, I will express a couple as direction

•   Tone of their face, has it changed variety? The eyebrows would they say they are striking or lose? Their eyes, would they say they are looking irate, agile or cheerful? (This is one that, as far as I can tell, some people have a hard time reading.) • The sound of their reaction, or the absence of it, is it hesitant? Or then again peaceful? Or then again irate? Etc...

•   Search for actual development, would they say they are squirming or utilizing portions of their body to contain themselves? Or on the other hand to put themselves out there? Typically if you are enthusiastic about something you need to communicate, your face or arms/hands are the main body parts to move deliberately for you.

• Is their response more precise or less precise in terms of the words they chose and how quickly they elaborated? Is it surged or more satisfied?

As this stage there's no way around the timing, as you've executed it, everything without a doubt revolves around change. The main way you can change is by noticing and surveying. Assuming you won't do as such, the discussion might turn sour and it's the worst situation imaginable, except if you've deliberately gone down that course obviously.

• Your tone, utilizing a gentler pitch could assist with moving your direction back into the people regard and pardoning

• The speed at which you talk, you might need to stop somewhat more tune in and afterward have a 'determined' think and stand up just when you're prepared.

• Your trustworthiness, on the off chance that you've gone in erroneously with wrong realities or suspicions, you conceding your wrong is definitely not something terrible. Recall the discussion is two way, on the off chance that you've made the best decision and they don't invite it then the next move is up to them to change not you.

In general, your timing as referenced is your multiplier, the more exertion you put in toward the beginning; the more likely it is that your strategy will succeed. You should depend on a couple of human abilities which differ with each person, for example, noticing, judging and surveying what is happening.

I mentioned grace and forgiveness earlier when two people were talking face to face. However, if you were communicating via email or message and the content was written in an aggressive tone or with incorrect facts, the natural response would be to be less gracious and more defensive, with a hint of vengeance in some cases. However in the event that a similar misstep was made eye to eye the elegance and pardoning levels are a lot higher.

The connection among time and correspondence

Time is a scant and important asset that impacts how you convey and how others see your messages. At the point when you are feeling the squeeze, you might feel hurried, focused, or overpowered, which can influence your capacity to design, sort out, and convey your correspondence. You might also have less time to listen to your audience, respond to them, and follow up, which could hurt your rapport and feedback. Then again, when you deal with your time well, you can impart all the more smoothly, actually, and powerfully, as well as construct trust and believability with your crowd.

Dealing with your time well can be extremely valuable for working on your correspondence under tension. It permits you to focus on undertakings and spotlight on the most significant and critical issues. Also, it offers you the chance to assign sufficient opportunity to plan, research, and practice your correspondence. In addition, it assists you with keeping away from dawdling, interruption, and interference that can adversely influence the quality and clearness of your correspondence. Moreover, it empowers you to set reasonable and clear assumptions and cutoff times for you as well as your crowd, as well as convey them actually. At last, it empowers you to adjust your correspondence responsibility and stay balanced, exhaustion, and dissatisfaction that can debilitate your relational abilities.

COMMITMENT AND CONSISTENCY

The responsibility and consistency rule is a strong mental instrument that can assist you with impacting others and accomplish your objectives. In light of the thought individuals will generally act in manners that are steady with their past responsibilities, particularly assuming they are made freely or deliberately. By utilizing this guideline, you can convince others to concur with you, help out you, or backing you in different circumstances. Use the commitment and consistency principle to influence others in the following effective ways.

Begin little

One method for utilizing the responsibility and consistency standard is to begin with a little solicitation or favor that is simple for the other individual to acknowledge. This can make a feeling of responsibility or correspondence, and make them bound to consent to a bigger or more significant solicitation later on. For instance, in the event that you believe somebody should give to your goal, you can initially request that they sign an appeal, wear an identification, or offer a post. This can cause them to feel more lined up with your objective and more ready to give when you ask them.

One more method for utilizing the responsibility and consistency rule is to utilize social evidence, which is the propensity of individuals to follow the way of behaving or assessments of others, particularly assuming they are comparative or powerful. By showing that others have previously dedicated to your thought, item, or administration, you can build the believability and engaging quality of your proposition, and cause the other individual to feel more certain and agreeable to participate. For instance, assuming that you believe somebody should purchase your item, you can show them tributes, appraisals, or supports from different clients or specialists.

A third method for utilizing the responsibility and consistency rule is to make a feeling of shortage, which is the insight that something is interesting, important, or restricted. By suggesting that your proposition is popular, low stockpile, or going to terminate, you can set off an apprehension about passing up a major opportunity, and make the other individual more anxious to commit before it is past the point of no return. For instance, assuming that you believe somebody should pursue your course, you can let them know that there are a couple of spots left, that the cost will go up soon, or that the enlistment cutoff time is drawing closer.

A fourth method for utilizing the responsibility and consistency rule is to be steady yourself, and that implies that you act in manners that are consistent with your words, values, and convictions. Thusly, you can lay out trust, believability, and authority, and make the other individual more open and conscious to your messages. For instance, assuming you believe somebody should heed your guidance, you can show them that you have followed it yourself, that you have significant experience or capabilities, or that you have positive outcomes or results.

A fifth method for utilizing the responsibility and consistency standard is to convince them, and that implies that you make sense of why you are making your solicitation, proposition, or idea, and how it will help them or others. Thusly, you can engage their rationale, feelings, or values, and make them more spurred and convinced to concur with you. For instance, on the off chance that you believe somebody should join your group, you can let them know how they will master new abilities, meet new individuals, or have an effect.

A 6th method for utilizing the responsibility and consistency rule is to permit them some opportunity, and that implies that you don't pressure them to an extreme, or cause them to feel caught or controlled. Thusly, you can regard their independence, inclinations, and feelings, and make them bound to commit willfully and truly. For instance, assuming that you believe somebody should change their way of behaving, you can give them a few choices, options, or motivators, as opposed to dangers, ultimatums, or disciplines.

CREDIBILITY – BEING AUTHENTIC

Believability is fundamental for employing power successfully, as it frames the premise of a pioneer's capacity to impact others. Factors like straightforwardness, responsibility, uprightness, and vision are critical to building believability, which thus improves a pioneer's power. A strong pioneer can enable others by sharing their power, in this manner acquiring more noteworthy impact over others and accomplishing hierarchical objectives all the more successfully. In business, power requires credibility and the ability to project it through appearance, behavior, and behavior. Extraordinary pioneers become progressively more valid, which improves their power. The developing power, when practiced appropriately, increments validity, which thus upgrades power. It's a temperate circle.

Believability is actually the foundation of Force. You lose believability and you lose power, the capacity to impact others. Furthermore, obviously, the inverse is likewise evident, the more solid you are, the almost certain you can impact others and that is Power. Once more, extraordinary chiefs impact others they have validity. They stand by listening to other people, they accept info and exhortation, they learn, and they sell their groups or workers. They seldom urge. Extraordinary pioneers and influential individuals get "purchase in". They can get others to accept possession also. This quite often is more effective than "requesting" somebody to follow through with something.

Validity

Validity alludes to being persuading, convincing, and trusted. Believability comes from great work propensities — understanding what is required, finishing tasks on time, clearing the air regarding challenges, and being a cooperative person.

Believability additionally comes from giving strong proof to help proposals. At last, earnestness improves validity actually intending what you say and keeping away from work environment tattle. Validity is an essential for impact and power.

Impact

Impact is the capacity to affect someone else or an arranging result.

One sort of impact comes from the power allowed in the position. An organizer investigating improvement applications, for instance, impacts the understanding of drafting and development guidelines. Plan-authors impact the substance, association, and language of the plans.

Impact, be that as it may, is more than the specialists conceded to a position. A lesser organizer can impact their manager by proposing imaginative suggestions, upheld by proof and examination. By inspiring and encouraging others, a team member can exert influence. Impact can be likewise acquired in an organization, for example, an inner city group or coordinated effort with specialist co-ops. Persuasive organizers foster organizations as they work.

POWER

Power is the capacity to change the way of behaving of others or decide results in plan-production and execution. It is a disagreeable word for some, as it appears to be in conflict with the ideal of populist groups, coordinated effort, and correspondence.

In the event that it isn't recognized, however, power might be as yet working underneath the surface. Power is to some degree characterized by position portrayals and association diagrams, however that isn't the main variable. Power requires validity and impact. This is shown when two organizers with a similar position portrayal have various degrees of force.

How do power, influence, and credibility relate to one another?

The base for this threesome is validity; impact and power ordinarily develop from that. Building validity resembles making a retirement account, setting aside customary installments, keep away from withdrawals, and exploiting compounding.

Ordinary stores are top notch work and exhibit of good person, withdrawals are intermittent errors, and compounding is the synergistic improvement of your standing over the long haul. Validity is uncovered when you are looked for guidance and can tackle issues with others. This procedure cannot be completed in a hurry.

Impact is gotten from believability. It doesn't simply mean getting everything you could possibly want, obviously, in light of the fact that even humbly steering an arranging exertion or choice can be an achievement. Regardless of whether a choice conflicts with your proposal, the following arranging choice might be founded on endeavors in the past case.

The individuals who have impact are practical about how interests are adjusted and consider cautiously about how to utilize that leverage. It is something that compelling organizers support, secure, and wisely use, cautiously taking into account where and when to utilize it.

Power amazes and is important to battle for a long term benefit: to oppose debasement, accomplish civil rights, advance manageability, or quite a few arranging objectives. Yet, it can likewise mislead an organizer.

Successful organizers utilize the power they have with a light touch. It comes from formal position portrayals, a capacity to team up and shape alliances, and one's validity and impact.

SCARCITY

A potent psychological principle, scarcity can motivate others to take action, increase their value of something, or feel motivated. In view of the thought individuals need what is uncommon, restricted, or selective, and dread passing up open doors or assets.

Figure out the sorts of shortage

There are two principal kinds of shortage that you can use to impact others: amount shortage and time shortage. Amount shortage alludes to the restricted accessibility or supply of something, like an item, a help, a prize, or an asset. Time shortage alludes to the restricted span or cutoff time of something, like a proposition, an occasion, a choice, or an objective.

The two kinds of shortage can make a need to get moving, contest, and restrictiveness that can make others more intrigued, inquisitive, and able to act.

Shortage can be an incredible asset, yet it can likewise blow up in the event that you use it unscrupulously or manipulatively. You run the risk of losing trust, credibility, and reputation if you create artificial or false scarcity, such as by lying about the number of items left. Individuals can undoubtedly distinguish trickery or irregularity, and they will feel cheated, angry, or furious assuming that they find out. Thusly, use shortage with genuineness and trustworthiness, and just when it is valid, significant, and valuable for the two players.

Pick the perfect proportion of shortage

Shortage can have various impacts relying upon how much shortage you make. Too little shortage can cause something to appear to be excessively normal, simple, or modest, and lessen its apparent worth or allure. An excess of shortage can cause something to appear to be excessively troublesome, hazardous, or costly, and increment its apparent expense or exertion. The ideal measure of shortage is the one that makes a harmony among market interest, and among want and possibility. You need to make something sufficiently scant to set off interest and activity, yet not so scant that it deters or overpowers.

People can only be influenced by scarcity if they are aware of and comprehend it. As a result, you need to use concrete numbers, dates, or other specifics to convey scarcity in a clear and specific way. For instance, rather than saying "This proposition is just accessible temporarily", say "This deal lapses on Friday at 12PM". You can make scarcity more real, credible, and compelling by being clear and specific.

Shortage can be more powerful assuming you consolidate it with other mental rules that can upgrade its effect. For instance, you can utilize social confirmation to show how others are answering the shortage, like tributes, surveys, appraisals, or supports. You can utilize power to show how specialists or forces to be reckoned with are suggesting or utilizing the scant thing, like qualifications, grants, or supports. You can utilize correspondence to show how you are offering something important or supportive in return for the scant thing, like a free preliminary, a reward, or a markdown. By consolidating shortage with different standards, you can build trust, believability, and worth.

What is the Shortage Rule? According to the scarcity principle, you value something more when it is scarce.

Open doors appear to be more significant to us when their accessibility is restricted.

Have you at any point gone to purchase an item online just to have a ticking clock spring up, counting during the time you have passed on to complete the request?

Your pulse increments, Adrenaline begins siphoning through your veins. When you type in your credit card information quickly, you wonder how a tiny timer could have such a big effect on your body. What you feel is the scarcity principle at work.

It appears that a one-time event is more valuable than a weekly one.

Due to the scarcity principle, a "limited-edition"
sneaker is more sought after than the mainstream
version from last year.

Instances of the Shortage Standard

Money

Indeed, even the worth of money, similar to the U.S.
dollar or the digital money Bitcoin, is affected by the
quantity of them accessible.

One of Bitcoin's guiding principle recommendations
is that there will just at any point be 21million of
them. Furthermore, after each 'dividing,' (as less

Bitcoin become accessible) the cost has risen emphatically.

Sales Techniques I recently encountered a variant of it in a Pasadena, California, F45 gym. The rec center made some one-memories limited time half year rate that must be secured in after your top notch. On the off chance that my significant other and I didn't take the arrangement right away, the delegate guaranteed us it was long gone. (We didn't take it).

This "cutoff time" driven time limit method is a typical shortage strategy. It creates you esteem the open door all the more now since you can't get a similar arrangement later.

There's additionally the "set number" strategy, where you are informed that the item you need is restricted in amount. In the event that you don't buy now, there won't be any left for you to purchase later.

These strategies are intended to stun you into a similar condition of pressure as the internet ticking look at clock. This condition of shortage initiated pressure doesn't permit you a second to think sanely, and frequently finishes with you purchasing something.

Why we neglect to Overwhelm

1.   Being excessively Scary

2.   Constant Annoying/talking babble

3.   Misrepresenting our powerful abilities

4.   being excessively energetic

5.   Talking without tuning in

6.   being excessively restless

7.   Misreading your crowd

Methods for fostering your impacting abilities -

Here are a few pointers to assist you with further developing your impacting abilities:

Acquire the Trust of others - Acquiring your collaborators' trust sets you in a more grounded position to impact them. Here are a few systems for acquiring trust:

Be honest.

Be trustworthy.

Trust individuals.

2. Fabricate areas of strength for an organization

Organizing requires meeting and shaping associations with individuals in your business. A solid expert organization can help your standing, making others focus on what you need to say. You may presumably find and go to systems administration occasions in your field or contingent upon your aptitude level. You could possibly go to a systems administration occasion for youthful experts or a land organizing occasion, for instance.

3. Give constructive feedback. It's possible that giving constructive feedback will show others that you are willing to assist and have good ideas. Giving and receiving constructive feedback both require one to be able to accept criticism. In the work environment, criticism is useful since it prompts individual and business progress.

We should see more about Impacting Abilities

1. Meaning-

- Someone or something influence on another.

• The capacity of an individual or object to produce such effects.

•   Capacity, pay, position, and different elements add to power or control.

•   An individual or gathering with the ability to impact others is known as an impact.

2. Importance

•   Being an incredible communicator requires the capacity to impact others.

•   You as of now have normal abilities to impact, which you use accidentally.

•   Moving these abilities to your cognizant brain and reinforcing them can assist you with turning into a genuinely magnificent powerhouse.

• Rather than complaining about the state of affairs, influencing others means taking action.

- Individuals appreciate being in the organization of people who can impact others. Any errand becomes more straightforward when you can impact others.

A decent powerhouse continually conveys legitimately, smoothly, and without hesitation to rouse and motivate others by engaging their inert advantages. The influencer is able to extinguish the latent attraction in people by influencing them on a subconscious level.

3. Attributes of Good Force to be reckoned with-

- Fiery and energetic

- Have a quiet and calm person.

- Versatile and adaptable

- It is fundamental to Tune in and perception capacities.

- Capacity to act impartially or fair-mindedly

- Confidence

- Keen and Sympathetic

You should be vivacious and energetic if you have any desire to be a force to be reckoned with. You ought to keep a cool and loosened up approach and try not to flip out. A fruitful powerhouse should likewise be adaptable and adaptable. They ought to acknowledge the changes. Impact isn't just about what you say, it's likewise about how well you stand by listening to other people, notice them, and get things done for them that make them glad for you. Forces to be reckoned with ought to be impartial and unbiased, instead of one-sided. They should likewise be confident, merciful, and savvy.